KNOW THE STATS

BASEBALL

IS A NUMBERS GAME

by Eric Braun

CAPSTONE PRESS
a capstone imprint

Sports Illustrated Kids Know the Stats are published by Capstone Press,
a Capstone Imprint, 1710 Roe Crest Drive, North Mankato, Minnesota 56003.
www.mycapstone.com

Library of Congress Cataloging-in-Publication Data
is available on the Library of Congress website:
ISBN: 978-1-5435-0609-9 (library binding)
ISBN: 978-1-5435-0617-4 (eBook PDF)

Editorial Credits
Nate LeBoutillier, editor; Brent Slingsby, designer;
Eric Gohl, media researcher; Laura Manthe, production specialist

Photo Credits
Getty Images: Stringer/Ron Schwane, 25; Library of Congress: 21; Newscom: Icon Sportswire/
John Cordes, 15, Icon Sportswire/Mark Goldman, 11, Icon Sportswire/Patrick Gorski, 9, UPI/Pat
Benic, 26, USA Today Sports/Robert Deutsch, 5; Sports Illustrated: Damian Strohmeyer, 19, David E.
Klutho, cover, Heinz Kluetmeier, 23, John W. McDonough, 12, Robert Beck, 7, 16, 28

Design Elements: Shutterstock

All statistics have been updated through the 2017 MLB season.

Printed in the United States of America.
010782S18

TABLE OF
CONTENTS

STATS & STORIES

A Daring Dash

Baseball statistics can show everything from how fast a pitcher's curveball spins to what a batter's strengths and weaknesses are. Players use stats to figure out how best to beat an opponent. Teams use stats to decide how much a player's next contract is worth. Fans use stats to boast about their favorite players. Every stat tells a story.

Stats don't always tell the *whole* story, of course. Consider *this* story: In Game 5 of the 2015 World Series, the Kansas City Royals were losing 2-1 to the New York Mets. With one out in the ninth inning, Royals baserunner Eric Hosmer stood on third base. He was just 90 feet away from home plate and a tie game when a Royals batter hit a grounder to third baseman David Wright. Wright fielded the ball cleanly and checked Hosmer, who froze. But as soon as Wright looked away to throw to first, Hosmer broke for home.

The Mets first baseman was surprised by the gutsy move. He caught the ball for out number two and then fired it home — but his throw was high. Hosmer slid in to tie the game, and the Royals went on to win in extra innings.

Stats can't explain split-second thinking or show daring decisions. However, stats played a big role in Hosmer's choice. Hosmer knew that the Mets closer could throw sinkers at 97 miles an hour and had an earned run average of 1.85. Those numbers told Hosmer that the chances of the next Royals batter getting a hit were very slim. Thus Hosmer figured that bolting for home, even at the risk of making a game-ending out, was the best option.

The most important statistic of all says Hosmer was right: His team got the win. And Hosmer's dash helped the Royals go on to become World Series champions.

CHAPTER ONE

PITCHING

Strikeouts [Ks]

Steee-rike three!

Grab some bench, batter.

For a pitcher, strikeouts are a true show of dominance. They also give his team the best chance to win. It's pretty hard for your opponents to score if they can't put the bat on the ball.

For that reason, strikeout totals are a quick, easy way to measure a pitcher's value. If a pitcher piles up a lot of them, we know he's hard to hit — and hard to score on. That's why Los Angeles Dodgers hurler Clayton Kershaw is one of the most valuable pitchers in the game today.

In 2015 Kershaw struck out 301 batters over 232.2 innings. That was 25 more Ks than the next best National League (NL) pitcher that year. Kershaw also won the NL strikeout crown in 2011 and 2013. In both 2016 and 2017, he struggled with injuries. Though he missed parts of each season, he still finished with 172 and 200 Ks, respectively — excellent strikeout numbers.

Kershaw has already whiffed more than 2,000 batters since joining the big leagues in 2008. That puts him on the path to elite company.

Clayton Kershaw, pitcher,
L.A. Dodgers

Most Strikeouts, Career

Rank		Years Played
Rank: 01	Nolan Ryan	27
Rank: 02	Randy Johnson	22
Rank: 03	Roger Clemens	24
Rank: 04	Steve Carlton	24
Rank: 05	Bert Blyleven	22

01 5,714
02 4,875
03 4,672
04 4,136
05 3,701

Earned Run Average (ERA)

When the Chicago Cubs won it all in 2016, they had no shortage of heroes. Their pitching rotation was anchored by aces Jake Arrieta and Jon Lester. However, Kyle Hendricks was young and relatively unknown outside of Chicago. He'd pitched only 260 big-league innings in his first two years as a pro.

But in 2016 Hendricks had a monster season. He went from the fifth starter to super-starter. One stat shows just how good he was: He had the lowest earned run average in the league.

ERA is the average number of earned runs a pitcher gives up over a nine-inning game. To calculate ERA, first divide the number of earned runs allowed by the number of innings pitched. Then multiply the result by nine.

Kyle Hendricks ERA, 2016

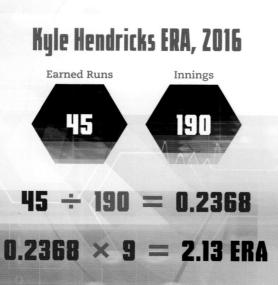

Earned Runs   Innings

45   **190**

$$45 \div 190 = 0.2368$$

$$0.2368 \times 9 = 2.13 \text{ ERA}$$

For every nine innings, Hendricks gave up just over two earned runs on average. That's a good formula for winning games.

Hendricks doesn't have a blazing fastball or a trick pitch. Rather, he relies on movement and control. It works for him. The proof is in the ERA.

Kyle Hendricks, pitcher, Chicago Cubs

Walks + Hits per Inning Pitched (WHIP)

What's the key to preventing runs? How about preventing baserunners? If nobody gets on base, nobody can cross home plate.

That's what WHIP measures — the number of baserunners a pitcher allows in an average inning. Along with ERA, it's a good stat for measuring a pitcher's performance. A pitcher with a low ERA but a high WHIP is playing with fire. He's allowing a lot of baserunners, and some of them are bound to score sooner or later.

To calculate WHIP, add up all the walks and hits a pitcher allows. Then divide that number by the number of innings he pitched. Take a look at Baltimore closer Zach Britton's 2016 WHIP.

Zach Britton WHIP, 2016

Innings Pitched
67

Walks
18

Hits
38

Add **18** plus **38** to get the number of baserunners Britton allowed that year: **56**.

Then divide **56** by **67**, his innings pitched:

$$56 \div 67 = 0.836 \text{ WHIP}$$

Britton allowed less than a baserunner per inning. He was so dominant in 2016 that he made the rare strong case for winning the Cy Young Award as a reliever (though he did not win).

Zach Britton, pitcher, Baltimore Orioles

Francisco Rodriguez, pitcher,
L.A. Angels of Anaheim

Saves (S)

There's no worse feeling than losing a game that you were leading until the very end. It's like a punch to the gut. That's why teams often bring in a fresh pitcher to finish out games that they're leading. These pitchers, known as closers, usually throw serious gas. They come in to burn through that last inning — and "save" the day.

Some of the greatest relievers in history have earned their fame by collecting bundles of saves. In 2008 closer Francisco Rodriguez got 62 saves for the Los Angeles Angels — setting the single season record.

The save is given to the pitcher who finishes a close win. A pitcher is awarded a save if he finishes the victory but is not credited with the win. In addition one of the following three things must be true:

- He enters the game with a lead of no more than three runs and pitches for at least one inning.
- He enters the game with the potential tying run on base, at bat, or on deck.
- Or he pitches for at least three innings.

Saves Leaders, Career

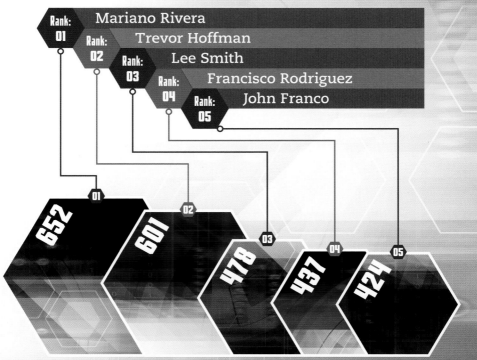

Rank	Player	Saves
01	Mariano Rivera	652
02	Trevor Hoffman	601
03	Lee Smith	478
04	Francisco Rodriguez	437
05	John Franco	424

CHAPTER TWO

HITTING

Batting Average [BA]

Some baseball statistics just seem to have a magical ring to them. A particular number will carry the weight of history. It symbolizes a great moment or an incredible feat.

One such number is a .400 batting average.

Batting average gives a quick snapshot of a player's hitting ability. You just take the number of hits a player gets, and then divide it by his number of at bats. The answer you get is a decimal that's usually displayed to the third digit. For example, in 2017 Houston Astros second baseman Jose Altuve had a .346 average, best in the American League. In 2016 Altuve got 216 hits out of 640 at bats.

Jose Altuve's Batting Average, 2017

$$204 \div 590 = .346$$

So what's the magic about .400? In nearly 80 years, no major league player has gotten a batting average of .400 or better. The last man to do it was Red Sox great Ted Williams, who hit .406 in 1941. A few batters have challenged the record through the early months of a season. But they usually fade by the end of the year. Perhaps Altuve has the best shot to reach .400 in the modern era.

Jose Altuve, second baseman, Houston Astros

Batting Average Leaders, 2011-2017

Year	Player	Team (League)	Average
2011	Miguel Cabrera	Tigers (AL)	.344
2011	Jose Reyes	Mets (NL)	.337
2012	Miguel Cabrera	Tigers (AL)	.330
2012	Buster Posey	Giants (NL)	.336
2013	Miguel Cabrera	Tigers (AL)	.348
2013	Michael Cuddyer	Rockies (NL)	.331
2014	Jose Altuve	Astros (AL)	.341
2014	Justin Morneau	Rockies (NL)	.319
2015	Miguel Cabrera	Tigers (AL)	.338
2015	Dee Gordon	Marlins (NL)	.333
2016	Jose Altuve	Astros (AL)	.338
2016	DJ LeMahieu	Rockies (NL)	.348
2017	Jose Altuve	Astros (AL)	.346
2017	Charlie Blackmon	Rockies (NL)	.331

Mike Trout, outfielder, L.A. Angels of Anaheim

On-Base Percentage [OBP]

Mike Trout might be the best player in the major leagues today. He plays terrific defense. He hits the ball a lot, and he hits it hard. But he has another skill that is not as obvious — though it is just as important. He has a high on-base percentage.

The percentage of the time that a batter gets on base is OBP. Like batting average, it is represented by a three-digit decimal. If you come to bat ten times and get on base four times, you have an OBP of .400. But unlike batting average, OBP gives batters credit for getting on base any way they can — including by walk.

A batter with a good eye gets more walks. Speed also plays an important role in OBP. A fast runner can turn infield grounders into hits by beating out throws to first.

So why is OBP so important? If you're on base a lot, you have more chances to score. The stat of OBP has taken on greater value in recent seasons as those who study the game take a closer look at the numbers.

OBP Leaders, 2017

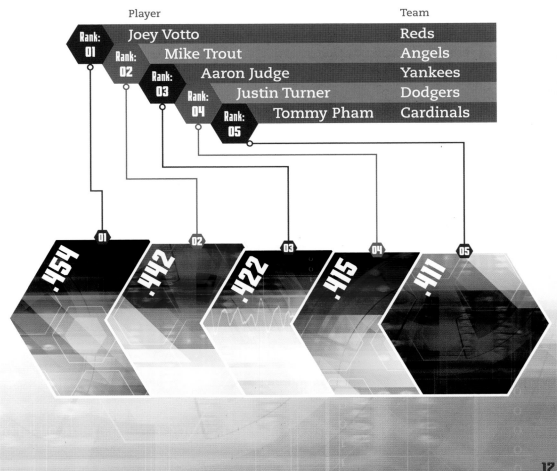

Player		Team
Rank: 01	Joey Votto	Reds
Rank: 02	Mike Trout	Angels
Rank: 03	Aaron Judge	Yankees
Rank: 04	Justin Turner	Dodgers
Rank: 05	Tommy Pham	Cardinals

01 .454
02 .442
03 .422
04 .415
05 .411

On-Base Plus Slugging (OPS)

Batting average measures a player's ability to get hits. OBP measures his ability to get on base. But what if you want a statistic that shows the bigger picture? In that case, your tell-all stat might be on-base plus slugging. OPS measures a hitter's ability to get on base *and* hit for power — the two main hitting skills.

To calculate OPS, you need to know the player's OBP and his slugging percentage (SLG). Slugging percentage is a measure of a hitter's power. It tells you how many bases a batter gets on average for each at bat. An SLG of .620 means a batter averages about 62 percent of a base per time up.

In 2016 David Ortiz had one of his best seasons in a career loaded with great seasons. His OPS shows just how good it was. Ortiz's OPS was tops in baseball that year and the fourth best of his career.

David Ortiz OPS, 2016

OBP .401   SLG .620

.401 + .620 = 1.021

OPS 1.021

Highest OPS, Career

Rank: 01	Babe Ruth
Rank: 02	Ted Williams
Rank: 03	Lou Gehrig
Rank: 04	Barry Bonds
Rank: 05	Jimmie Foxx

01 1.1636
02 1.1155
03 1.0798
04 1.0512
05 1.0376

David Ortiz, designated hitter, Boston Red Sox

Home Runs (HR)

Going, going . . . gone!

Though pitchers would probably disagree, there is something beautiful about a home run. Whether it's a towering moonshot or a laser line drive, the home run is pure power — with emphasis on the *POW*.

Home runs are a simple statistic to track. Just add them up. Yankees slugger Babe Ruth was the original home run king. He led the league in homers for 12 seasons. And his career mark of 714 dingers stood from 1935 until April 8, 1974. That's when Hank Aaron of the Atlanta Braves knocked his 715th career bomb, making him the all-time leader. Aaron retired with 755 career home runs. That record stood until Barry Bonds of the San Francisco Giants broke it on August 7, 2007.

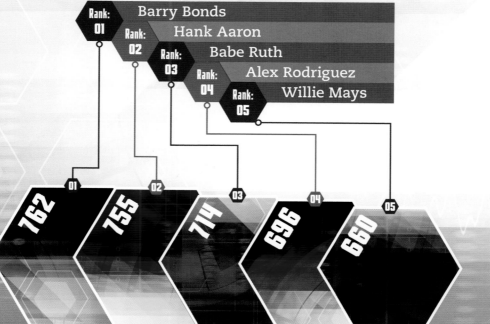

Home Run Leaders, Career

Rank	Player	HR
01	Barry Bonds	762
02	Hank Aaron	755
03	Babe Ruth	714
04	Alex Rodriguez	696
05	Willie Mays	660

The closest we've seen anyone come to the record recently was New York Yankee Alex Rodriguez. A-Rod retired after the 2016 season with 696 career homers. Albert Pujols of the Los Angeles Angels has a chance to overtake him. He's hit more than 600 homers, and he's probably got a few more years to play.

Babe Ruth, slugger, New York Yankees

Stolen Bases [SB]

In today's MLB, the stolen base has gone out of style. But not too long ago, fans loved watching speedsters like Tim Raines and Rickey Henderson swipe bags nearly every day. Between 1980 and 1983, Henderson stole more than 100 bases in three out of four seasons. In 2016 the entire Baltimore Orioles team stole only 19 bases all year.

Today stolen bases have become less popular because teams have decided the risk is too high. With more hitters able to blast extra-base hits, the smart choice is to play it safe and wait for the big hit.

But sometimes a stolen base makes a huge difference. In the 2004 American League Championship Series, the Boston Red Sox were facing elimination against their rivals, the Yankees. Down by one in the bottom of the ninth inning, Kevin Millar coaxed a walk against excellent Yankees closer Mariano Rivera. The Red Sox brought in a pinch runner for Millar — the speedy David Roberts.

Most Stolen Bases, Career

Rank	Player	SB
01	Rickey Henderson	1,406
02	Lou Brock	938
03	Billy Hamilton	914
04	Ty Cobb	897
05	Tim Raines	808

Right: Rickey Henderson, outfielder, Oakland Athletics
Left: Paul Molitor, infielder, Milwaukee Brewers

Everyone knew Roberts was going to try to steal second. Even so, Roberts swiped it. When third baseman Bill Mueller got a base hit to center field, Roberts came all the way around to score and tie the game! The Sox ended up winning on a David Ortiz homer in the bottom of the 12th. They then went on to win the next seven games in a row, knocking off the Yankees and sweeping the St. Louis Cardinals in the World Series.

And it almost certainly wouldn't have happened without that one stolen base.

CHAPTER THREE

FIELDING

Errors (E)

The traditional way to measure a defender's ability is with errors. The idea is simple. If the scorer thinks the defender should have made a play that he didn't, that defender is given an error. A player who rarely makes errors is considered a strong defender.

But sometimes it's not so obvious if the player should have made a play. Bias can also influence decisions. In other words, a scorer's judgment is not always perfect.

Another problem is that errors only measure mistakes. They don't tell you anything about great plays that players make on the field.

Most Errors Committed, 2017

Rank	Player	Team	Errors
01	Tim Anderson	White Sox	28
02	Dansby Swanson	Braves	20
02	Orlando Arcia	Brewers	20
02	Nicholas Castellanos	Tigers	20
02	Tim Beckham	Rays	20

Tie

Here's an example. On May 14, 2017, Cleveland first baseman Carlos Santana hit a line drive deep into center field. Minnesota Twins centerfielder Byron Buxton got a good read and seemed to fly across the grass. He managed to snag the ball just before crashing into the wall. He lost his glasses and cap but held on to the ball for the out.

For that incredible play, he didn't get an error. But he also didn't get credit for making an amazing catch. That's why errors are only one small part of the picture when evaluating defense.

Byron Buxton, outfielder, Minnesota Twins

Ultimate Zone Rating (UZR)

Here's a stat that does more than just count mistakes on the field. Ultimate zone rating divides the field into zones. Then it looks at all the plays fielders make and don't make in each zone. Players get more credit for catches made in zones farther from their beginning position. They lose credit for missing plays in closer zones.

It's complicated to compute UZR, but it's easy to understand. Simply put, UZR is shown as a number of runs saved or lost. A UZR of zero is average. A negative UZR means you are costing your team runs. A positive score means you're saving runs and helping your team.

Francisco Lindor, infielder, Cleveland Indians

Cleveland shortstop Francisco Lindor had a UZR of 20.8 in 2016. That means he saved his team 20.8 runs compared to an average shortstop. His stellar defense is a big reason his team made it all the way to Game 7 of the World Series.

Only three players had a better UZR than Lindor in 2016. One of them was another shortstop, Brandon Crawford of the Giants. He edged Lindor with a 21.3 UZR. Crawford is considered by many to be the best shortstop in the game. Which player would you rather have?

Does your opinion change when you read that Lindor had a .794 OPS compared to Crawford's .772? (See page 18.)

Highest UZR, 2016

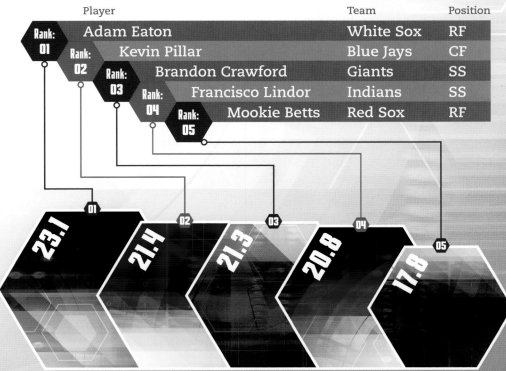

Rank	Player	Team	Position	UZR
01	Adam Eaton	White Sox	RF	23.1
02	Kevin Pillar	Blue Jays	CF	21.4
03	Brandon Crawford	Giants	SS	21.3
04	Francisco Lindor	Indians	SS	20.8
05	Mookie Betts	Red Sox	RF	17.8

Runs Above Average (RAA)

Many baseball fans and analysts consider catcher
to be the most important position on the field. But how
can you measure what catchers do? They hardly ever
field batted balls. Yet they handle the ball on nearly
every other play.

One new way of looking at catchers' defense is
pitch framing. Pitchers do the work of throwing balls
and strikes. But umpires aren't perfect. Sometimes
they make mistakes. Some balls are called strikes. And
some strikes are called balls.

However, catchers can influence strike calls with the way they catch the ball. A good catcher can make borderline pitches look more like a strike to the umpire. Giants catcher Buster Posey is one of the best at doing this.

Pitch framing stats look at how good catchers are at getting strikes called by the umpire. If you get a few extra strikes per game, it can add up to a difference in runs scored. That difference is described as runs above average.

Best Runs Above Average, 2016

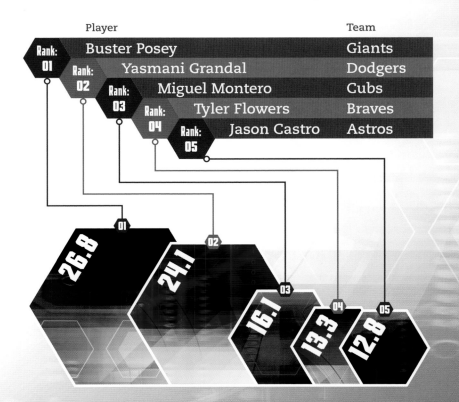

	Player	Team	
Rank: 01	Buster Posey	Giants	26.8
Rank: 02	Yasmani Grandal	Dodgers	24.1
Rank: 03	Miguel Montero	Cubs	16.1
Rank: 04	Tyler Flowers	Braves	13.3
Rank: 05	Jason Castro	Astros	12.8

GLOSSARY

earned run—a run scored without the help of an error in the field

Earned Run Average (ERA)—a statistic used to measure a pitcher's effectiveness; represents the number of earned runs a pitcher allows per nine innings

error—a baseball judgment given to a fielder who fails to convert an out on a play that an average fielder should have made

On-Base Percentage (OBP)—statistic measuring how frequently a batter reaches base per plate appearance

On-Base Plus Slugging (OPS)—statistic measuring how well a hitter can reach base and hit for average and power

pitch framing—the ability of a catcher to get more strikes called for his pitcher

Runs Against Average (RAA)—statistic measuring the number of runs above or below average that a player contributes to his team

slugging percentage—the average number of bases a batter gets per at bat; calculate by adding up total bases and dividing by number of at bats

save—statistic awarded to the relief pitcher who finishes the game for the winning team in which he holds onto a lead and meets other certain conditions

starter—a pitcher who starts games (as opposed to a relief pitcher)

Ultimate Zone Rating (UZR)—statistic measuring fielding; calculated by putting a run value on defensive ability to cover an area of the field

Walks and Hits per Inning Pitched (WHIP)—statistic measuring pitching ability; calculated by adding a pitcher's walks and hits divided by his total innings pitched

READ MORE

Braun, Eric. *Baseball Stats and the Stories Behind Them*. North Mankato, Minn.: Capstone Press, 2016.

Braun, Eric. *Pro Baseball's Underdogs: Players and Teams Who Shocked the Baseball World*, North Mankato, Minn.: Capstone Press, 2017.

Editors of Sports Illustrated Kids. *Big Book of WHO Baseball*, Sports Illustrated, 2017.

INTERNET SITES

Use FactHound to find internet sites related to this book.

Visit **www.facthound.com**

Just type in **9781543506099** and go.

Check out projects, games and lots more at
www.capstonekids.com

INDEX